# innocence

Deep

MOUNTAIN ARBOR
PRESS
Alpharetta, GA

ISBN: 978-1-6653-0251-7 - Paperback
eISBN: 978-1-6653-0252-4 - eBook

Library of Congress Control Number: 2021912267

Printed in the United States of America          0 6 1 8 2 1

∞This paper meets the requirements of ANSI/NISO Z39.48-1992 (Permanence of Paper)

# innocence

Dedicated to my Bibi, my grandmother Surjit Kaur.

I never stopped remembering that day and never will.

I am still on that school bus waiting for you.


You are in my heart for eternity.

A guide on how to get lost

This book has no rules

Write or draw wherever and however you like!

Read it in silence, out loud, with music or however you would like.

No rules here!

Ask yourself

How do I experience life if I can't hear or see?

Let yourself drift to this space and time

Enjoy the journey

In life innocence is lost every day, every moment.

What is innocence?

Perhaps our natural expression, the connection to the deepest depths of our entire selves.

Perhaps a recollection of parts of ourselves we hid and protected from the world.
Not the selves that have evolved from the changes from this world and life but the selves that existed before the change.

Change is often seen as the only constant but it is not. Perhaps this will be viewed as an attempt to recreate the past, it is not.

The past is there somewhere.

Yet your innocence is everywhere, in every space and time you exist, permeate and evolve in.

Innocence is also a constant in this life just like change.

Maybe Innocence is the essence behind change itself.

Protecting this connection to one's innocence can also protect the innocence of life itself and those in and out of it.

# Chapter 1
# The Unknown

After ten years of not

writing or expressing


My heart

burst open

In tears

The sky offers a lesson

Every day

&

Every night

Everything begins and ends

innocence

Why must we live in shells

And not share our hearts

With each other?

Why do we run from innocence

This sweetness within each of our hearts

Why do we not show this compassion

In every heart beat

Every interaction

Why not embrace this love

That we have for each other but still won't fully express

We will not live forever

I repeat

We will not live forever

You may never hear that voice, with that face and energy

All of the things you love about this person

Yet can't seem to fully show

Can't seem to say the words

I love you

The planets swim in

Space


As we drift and float


In our rhythms


Maybe the tears are the

Secret esoteric gateway

innocence

When the awareness that death will come one day arrives

No direction is lost or found

Where are you?

innocence

When do we spend unbroken

Time and space

With just ourselves ?

innocence

Often as humans we are not taught to embrace ourselves and our personal existence.

Instead we as men, women, children and adolescents of all ages and genders are taught to listen to the voices of others.

Not our internal voice but the voices of others. These voices drown our voice as children.

The innocence

**The unknown symbol**

Hold onto you for some time

And then I shall let you go


This is what life whispers into my ears

Listening


I also hold on for some time

And then let go

innocence

Is the breath inside of you different then the breath inside of me?

Listening with attention and surrender to the breath

All of life has become a meditation

You grow old not wise

when you

cease to

dream

**Afraid to say**

For a long time I was afraid to speak

Afraid of the sound that would leak

Wisdom was what I needed to seek but instead I let the judgment of

others smoother me into a

Dark hole

everything here yet gone

Deep

Yeah right, what's wrong is what I thought to myself

Why can't I speak, think and link my inner thoughts to this external

world?

Yet the mystery remained

I realized later that this one experience at that specific time allowed me

to understand the emptiness that exists in life

An emptiness that is hidden away due to human activity

Yet when everything seizes

The silence flows into your ears and at that moment it is you alone no

longer connected with anyone but yourself

Tears may roll down your eyes from this bizarre experience but the

more you

embrace it the more you begin to realize that this silence is not

what is hurting you or causing you pain.

But in fact it is your brain's constant push and drive to make everything

favorable and controllable for a structured existence

that leads to the mental, physical, and emotional pain that this uncertain

silence causes

An uncertainty which is an element of life that we as humans constantly

ignore or purposely neglect and overlook.

11

innocence

Let the innocence

return


It never left

You just lost the connection

Perhaps due to the projections

of others


Remember and unite

like the sight

of the intensity within the eyez

of lovers

forced apart

Are these lovers only on the outside or also within us?


Obliterating even the subtleties of

ether, space, aether, time


Or whatever you want to call it.

There is much depth

In the darkness of the night


Transcendence and immanence

A space between

going and staying


To fly or to dwell

Maybe both for now

How can the unseen be seen?

The power of chance is profound yet so simple

The overarching influence that it carries over all of life is pure magic

Ineffable

All of the synchronicities that

merge and submerge

an orientation of knowing


To think is far from being

When did we stop staring at

The ocean

Up

Above us?

When people place themselves in one form

they befriend ignorance

Ignorant to their own constructed

limitations and potentials

Life's fragility is

without

justification

innocence

As I experience

I learn

about myself

innocence

**The branch that connects me to you**

Are we like those two trees

that connected their branches to one another

because they couldn't live without each other?

These two trees connected by nature

Just like how we met

by chance

by nature

Their symbolic union shows that they realized their selves

but grew together

their existence connected until

the end

The two became one

They became so imbedded in

Each other that they

became a part of

one another

Together they live


Will we be like those

two trees

one day?

innocence

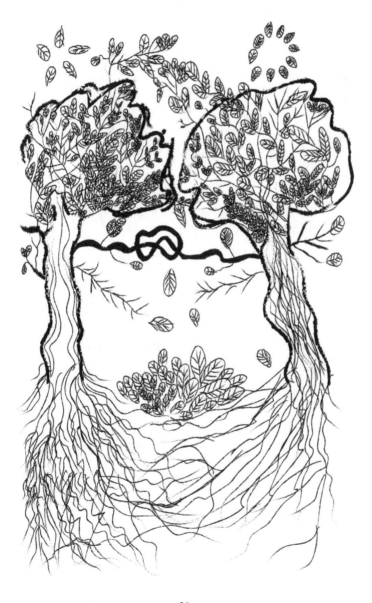

21
innocence

The wisdom of the elders is like the taste of honey

Cure yourself with this medicine

One day we too will age

&

If we have tasted even a bit of honey

We too will become elders

Cherish them while they are here like you would yourself

Take care of the elders as they have taken care of us

The arrival of the youth & the departure of the elders is

eternally interwined

22
innocence

| 1994 | 0 |
| 2006 | 1997 |
| 2010 | 1960 |
| 2012 | 1986 |
| 2016 | 2019 |
| 2017 | 1940 |
| 2018 | 2094 |
| 1996 | 3100 |
| 2020 | 2003 |

innocence

Cry

It is beautiful to cry

We don't need anyone's permission

There is no time or space inappropriate to feel so deeply and profoundly

Cry

It is beautiful to cry

You do not need external substances to express and feel your emotions and vulnerability.

Yes substances like ganja pull this out of you

There is wisdom in all forms of discovery

It is not always motivated by escapism

**Spring Nights**

Many memories if not most

become forgotten in the span of this life

Yet time is linear?

Year progresses after year

yet the memories of the moments of

those years

are gone from our mental realm

Or so it seems

with the same senses that we initially experience

we then forget and then with them

Perhaps like tonight as I am walking up this steep hill

A smell

reminds me

of family road trips

leaving at dawn

The few

very few trips that were taken

on rare occasions

Just like that in this presumably

Linear life

A collection

Entire collections of

Memories flood the moment

Or did they never leave

Waiting to be retrieved?

Senses are a pain

yet also a relief

Experience for yourself

No need to believe

It is not hoarding or attachment

But some memories

I would like to keep

close very close to

my heart

perhaps all

Before they truly fade like

The breath

Within

The soil that makes my earth body come to life

Breathe in

Breathe out

innocence

**Come inside and play**

Many don't understand the internal world

The infinite beauty of what is within


Unfortunately our eyes don't go inward

But does this keep us from exploring

the depth of what it means to be

me?

To be ourselves?

Irrespective of time or the external world?


The mystery

O Fellow humans


The mystery of what lies within is

The missing piece to understanding the beauty

of all the wonders

outside


Let the guard down

you are safe

here

unconditional existence

The realm that is

neither life or death


Perhaps this

This internal experience is eternity

Perhaps this is where we return to


Perhaps this is what

peace feels like

Feel don't think

Just feel the


mountains, valleys, oceans, deserts, jungles, meadows, forests,

marshes and volcanoes

within


There

Here is your oasis

**Breathe**

Breathing in

Breathing out

The simple reflection on respiration is turned profound

The mystic within awakens

How we take this magical breath for granted

How do we take this life giving breath for granted?

Perhaps just like how we take the water

 that fills more than half our bodies for granted

Or the food that turns into the skin and body that we live in

Nothing mere about this internal detection

hidden within us

the magic is us

How sacred it is

Sacred – a level of gratitude that causes one to surrender

unknowingly

How we forget this breath yet remember and identify with

thoughts, emotions and experiences

Breath flowing freely in time and space while roaming this

beautifully adorned home

Until the time and space is up

Is the breath not us?

Is our internal breathe any different from the external breeze?

This breath is us

Don't forget this breath

regardless of life experiences

Try to remember this mystical essence

the first and last bonds with this beautiful

existence

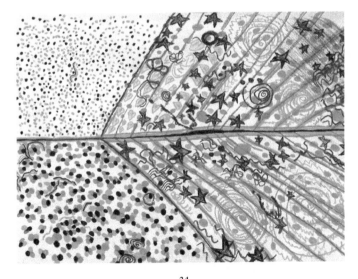

innocence

Before the big death

Life offers a series of mini deaths

Giving us opportunities to express depth through loss

While still here in life

Living

How beautiful of an experience this is

That life offers us

To grieve and embrace the unknown

innocence

A cataclysm emerges in the evergreen

Have you ever watched the sunset and sunrise?

Watching the motions of the sun

Even the smallest hints of fire create warmth

Regardless of the distance

Or the depths of the cold

innocence

**To You –To Me**

This body

O how beautiful this body is

Grateful to reside in this place I call home

The paradox of this home fading one day

Or maybe presently as I or something profound in this existence

helps me write

But just feel how beautiful it is here

Here in this beautiful body of yours

How much pain this body has weathered

The pain, ambitions and passions this body has supported you in

The endless moments of existence this body has continuously

allowed itself to stay solid in like a tree even when it's very being

is that of water

That of change

This body houses the vast dimensions of what we know to be us

and our reality

Cherish the body

Love it

Give your body a hug right now

Kiss it

Massage it

Feel those muscles & bones that you continuously strengthen & stretch

Don't just go building or destroying

Just chill with your body

Chill and enjoy what it means

to be

Massage away the pain that may be

present from the past


Kiss the tops of your right and left hands


Recognizing the commitment this body has made to support you

infinitely

Even when you lost faith in this relationship


The first relationship you came into this world with


Humbly bowing down with all of your spirit, mind and soul

Bask in the waves within the oceans of vibrations uttered next

and say with the instrument that is your tongue


I am honored to spend the rest of my life with you

Thank you


With the depths of love that only this body knows how to access

I surrender to you

The infinite

innocence

The many paths one can walk in this life are vast

Vast as perhaps life herself

Each with its own element of chance

Endless possibilities and opportunities

Beginnings and endings without beginning or end

The fragility of even the present moment

As you read these words

and the path you walked on to get here

O how beautiful this life is

But equally strange

How the stranger that was

Now is known

Or unknown once more

You have to see your own value

Sometimes that's all you have

## Nurture Nature

Have you spent some time in nature today?

O how beautiful it is!

The countless lessons and moments of utter nurturance that nature

gives freely

Without anything expected in return

Except perhaps reciprocity

Reciprocity of discovering the healing properties in oneself like

those hidden in plain sight in nature.

This beautiful force and flow

Endless

Giving our lives meaning beyond comprehension

In return what do we as humans do?

Contradictions indeed we are

We abuse it

subtly or overtly

Systematically attempting to destroy that which will always find a

way to

regenerate

Appreciate it even if we won't be here forever

 The here and now

Climb these trees but please be gentle

Roam the many lands but don't forget what you take these steps on

Breathe the mystical air that is also you

Don't treat it with disrespect

Please don't

Crying he said

Please do not hurt that which is yourself.

Don't die not knowing this.

Embrace life

Embrace yourself

I'm not going to stay here forever

When does life or death ever give us that opportunity?

Humans always want more

Maybe we just need to be grateful for what we have

Instead of asking for more

Respect every body

Each body is it's own

A woman's body doesn't belong to a man or the man's society

Neither does a man's or child's

Each body is its own

Respect everybody

Time is ruthless

Feeling through the various time periods I have lived in and the
experiences they hold

I begin to realize how time just continues to pass

Without beginning or end

Yet this physical life and its mental & emotional associations don't have
specifically defined beginning or ends

The intensity of it all

There is no control in coming or going

The beauty of it inherent

Yet I am sad at times

Depths of sadness because time is ruthless

I don't want to go

I don't want to forget

Everything or anything


I love all of it

There is nothing I would want more than for life to continue to never
leave

Yet even this is a paradox

Because to make a statement of leaving would mean there is something
known of the unknown

Yet there is not

innocence

there perhaps never will be

In these particular senses we have at least

The emotions and the realm of intuition and its magic perhaps are

different

Vortexes to the unknown

Still time is ruthless

Yet my love is eternal

It always will be

It always has been

The love for everything

There is no right or wrong

When there is compassion for all

The mystery grows with every moment

every year that I am granted another day

Gliding in the mysteries of this world and myself

Love shines the brightest light

Here

Here in the moment to moment existence we call life

With all my heart

They say it never

Existed

Yet it does


Much like our lives


if there is no one to

recall and recount


I guess

All we do in this world is

Take, take, take

When all we need to do is

give

# Reactions & Natural Expression

The topic discussed here is Natural expression versus reactions; this piece is an introspection for each individual human being that reads and feels these words.

The difference is subtle and sometimes neglected but the implications are important to analyze. The root of the distortion to oneself is the constant interactions we have with others. Especially those that unconsciously or consciously project. Projection doesn't take the experience of the other into account; it is inherently a selfish expression onto the other. A parasitic interaction is the basis of this projection where the other projects their experience in search of validation.

This need for validation and confirmation has many roots and meanings but most of them are connected with a lack of natural expression and connection to oneself. Those that project are typically recipients of the projections from others in their lives. This isn't stated to place the blame on those that project because sometimes we are living contradictions but it is stated to initiate a dialogue of introspection as mentioned above. Of course in life everything leads to growth one way or another but questioning from where the growth or destruction of the former self comes from is vital as it is connected to either force or flow. The beauty and madness of this life is interwoven and intrinsic with the seen and the unseen; chaos and structure, the internal and external, and oneself and the other.

Natural expression is prioritizing your connection to yourself before you share yourself with others. Natural expression is not formed in connection with the experience of the other but instead bonded with that of one's truth. This is not the same as being ignorant of another's experience. In fact the experience of the other is understood in a deeply profound way because of the internal connection to oneself being the primary priority. The difference is that the experienceof the other isn't what shapes one's experience or perspective, instead what is natural within reaches expression to the intellect and the senses.

In contrast, the word reaction is explained in the definition of the english word itself. Reactions are based on the relationship to cause and effectwhich typically are in connection to a situation, occurrence, object or person outside one's self or one's direct experience. Typically the cause of the reaction is the projection of others and the effect is questioning one's truth. Where as one's truth was already contained within one's essence even if it wasn't intellectualized.

Judgment given based on the projection of what one human being views as right or wrong is presented as a universal even though it only involves the experience of one's internal perspective. Instead the truth of the other and the self could have been honored simultaneously. Those that project and engage in reactions whether consciously or unconsciously act as parasites in search of validation for their own lack of self-understanding and connection.

If you have encountered this experience at some point within yourself or in relation to others how did you feel? How did you move from this; did you consciously process it or ignore it and perpetuate it further?

Inherently the concept of projection as mentioned above is attached with the concept of reactions. The integrity of one's experience is lost in exchange to the irresponsibility of the experience of the other which lacks compassion, intuition, sympathy and sensitivity. Not only is this damaging to the other but also to the being that created the projection that led to the reaction itself.

Some say there are truths within each truth and that protecting this truth is equal to protecting life itself. Thus infringing on the innocence, the essence or the truth violates the sacred. Sacred is defined here as a gratitude so profound that it creates surrender within every aspect of one's existence. This level of gratitude is found within natural expression but is absent in projections and reactions.

Being in connection with either reactions or natural expression should not be confused with being open minded or close minded to the ideas, emotions, perspectives or experiences of others but instead as exploring the connection or disconnection to one's intuition. Strengthening the connection by placing value and significance on the internal voice before all others. Creating a space and time, a home that doesn't interfere with the communication with yourself; instead it heightens it to the utmost.

The destruction or preservation of the first and last friendship that we encounter in this world – ourselves

Remains in our hands.

We are our own teachers, we have the ability to learn from our experiences in such a way that knowledge that we never cognitively gathered or learned begins to flow into our consciousness, into the way we feel, think and speak.

Emotions are the root of this beautiful experience of tapping into natural expression. Emotions manifest a reality that allows us to reach the depth of every experience internally and externally. The final transformation and evolution of this emotional intelligence is intuition. The magic of intuition is beyond words.

Anything that is sacred will allow for the emotions to reach their full intensity of clarity. Yoga an ancient practice that still survives in the modern time and space is a science and way of expression that has profound abilities to regenerate this seemingly lost connection to oneself. Yoga is not a set of postures, breath patterns or set of rules. Unfortunately over time this has become the definition but it is not the whole nor origin. The origin of this practice is natural expression, reaching the depth of the union and connection with oneself. The concept of oneself may start with your body, mind, thoughts and emotions at first but as this union intensifies perhaps everything becomes one.

Who knows?

Perhaps those who allow for natural expression to take

innocence

birth instead of participating in a collection of human societies that operate off of projection and reactions will be the conscious result.

Part of the whole contained within yoga is the art of breath and postural alignments of the skeletal, nervous and muscular system of the entire body; including the brain and heart. Tapping into this practice can have profound implications for what some refer to as an awakening. But all of this is only possible where the sacred is present.

The modern context of yoga will destroy itself to give birth to what was the whole and union once long ago. With this new day and night natural expression will arise and so will the untold power of emotions.

When one connects to reactions and projections the suppression of one's beauty is the result. Suppression of all that you have to share with yourself, all of the potentials hidden within the layers of being truly vulnerable and in surrender. A life based in reaction is connected to suppression and searching for validation.

Knowingly or unknowingly never letting yourself and others grow.

Lets choose different,

Lets look within.

## Synchronicity

Synchronicity begins to happen frequently

When touch is lost

With the constructs

While connection is established to

that which was lost

not looking to be found

## Ramadan

Hold silence in conversations, the truth will be felt and revealed. Regardless if that silent conversation is within yourself or with others.

The power of silence is beyond articulation or comprehension because it is beyond the senses that we experience reality from. Silence is the ultimate teacher. Silence teaches you to honor your truth at all times regardless of the circumstances. This enables the dualities of feeling and expression. Feeling is a process of expressing internally while expression is typically taking the internal feeling process and sharing it with the external reality. Feeling and expression both enable growth instead of the stagnation that arises from feeding into suppression. It allows you to grow and learn with the vulnerability of your truth instead of disregarding it.

Interestingly enough it also provides a safe haven for others to participate in their truth regardless if they know how to honor and respect that space and time or not. The beauty of silence is that it allows you to surrender and protect yourself against the unconscious or conscious destructive projections and intentions of others when they arise and become present in the moment. All of the resistance that this world forced on you and how you took this burden and reacted in retaliation with further resistance is shattered in an instant. Silence is that powerful; the magic of silence works like the element of water that pervades our body, planet and is intrinsically bonded with life itself.

Reactions can't exist if silence is the mediator, the medicine and the meditation.

No need to look for peace, it is hidden in plain sound and sight in the silence and stillness of this existence.

Taste a bit of silence and feel how natural expression, feeling and peace wander within you and wherever you go.

**Floating Dandelion Seeds**

Come with me

Lets float

and explore

Like dandelions


Our hidden gems stored within us

The seed of peace protected

The bubble of aura taking us wherever we are meant to go

or end up by chance


Floating endlessly

or

Landing eventually

grounding with the earth

But first we shall

Fly and play with the air


Oblivious even if all of creation bears witness

to our flight.

innocence

## Diwali

When my eyes opened

wide open

the soul began to see

for what felt like the first time


Once where I found nothing and no one

Now dark definite moments and states crumbled


Time slipped and skipped space

The self buried deep within

Unaffected by the world met

The worldly self


Eyes began to close

Embracing the pain

Pain dimensions beyond this world

The sanity that surpassed the serenity of death


Now began to transform to new dimensions

with the medicine of meditation

Death

Everyone seems to fear it

Yet it is something we will all embrace

Regardless with open or closed arms

Time here is scarce

Yet sacred

**Trust**

When was trust shattered?

When were the moments of innocence trampled on

The vulnerability went unnoticed

The childlike yearning to connect extinguished like a flame within the heart

A flame that brought warmth

That created comfort and release

The flame that sparked a light that transformed a house into a home

When did this trust get taken for granted?

When did it stop regenerating miraculously?

Trust is an interesting concept; we can't trust anyone until we first trust ourselves.

Yet we can't trust ourselves fully or even come close to it if we have yet to explore what the self is. Returning back to the innocence that was lost in the chaos of this world. Retrieving the innocence that was mishandled and misunderstood by the situations and people that we have interacted or encountered in the little lives that we have.

Don't you miss the magic of what it felt like to wake up as a child with such a renewed view of the world?

Even if it just meant waking up, eating or seeing your loved ones.

innocence

Wasn't this beautiful?

Why would we think this has to be lost as we adhere to the concept of aging in a time and space that is beyond any perceptions or cognition?

When will you trust again - the question is where is the vortex of lost and found, time and space where your innocence resides?

innocence

**Shadows**

In this moment to moment existence we call life

Light shines from the dark

Shadows

Gifts from the sun

Blending and blurring what is

What was and what could be

Past, Present and Future

Time between the dreams

Dreamtime

Some perceive life as a dream

While others fixate on what comes next or came before

The moment hidden within the secret of secrets

O how my heart longs for you

The bittersweet longing

Upon fulfillment of

The unknown

there is fear that

The known will forever be lost

In the maze of whatever is this life, existence or any other word that can

come close to signify and communicate that which is beyond the senses

innocence

The paradox of not wanting to go but day by night feeling yourself

going somewhere which is not here

Holding on but to what and for whom?


O The immortality of love

The beauty is in the mystery of the mystery

But what happens when the mystery is revealed?

All my loved ones I never want to leave

Never to depart from one another

Embedded together forever

within the moment

Here there is eternity

Infinite possibilities and potentials

Yet the shadows still loom in the day from the light of the sun

and also in the dark of the night

Yet love changes all of this

Change itself changes

Time is ruthless

Feeling through the various time periods I have lived in and the

experiences they

hold

I begin to realize how time just continues to pass

Without beginning or end

innocence

Lay in the grass and touch it

As you did before

unfiltered

Remembering perhaps

The certainty of one day

Never being able to see this again

In this way


Cherish everything

while you still can

### As a man

As a man I have endured the lifelong experience of feeling the life around or within me in profound moving depths. Catalyzing me towards action or moments that turned into days of dwelling in these powerful oceans of emotions. Every tear that flows down from the eyes similar to the single drops of water that make up the ocean.

Learning to protect this depth by standing firm on my toes, ten toes down, for this vast bodily experience. The pain felt by others projected on me; having to deal with the consequences. Not all projections turn to be detrimental but nonetheless a projection. Something that wasn't you but tried to become you.

Now after years of protecting my heart and the nature of feeling elements of the internal and external in depths that even the word introspection can't articulate; I find challenge.

Challenge to unlock the chains on this forced self-imprisonment. Protecting myself from those outside now also protecting myself from the inside.
My tendencies for violence and rage have developed for moments, days and years.

Here in this land

innocence

A jungle

That has been scorched barren as the desert

I now surrender

Bringing the depth and balance of stillness and chaos

Of the oceans within

Pouring outward to nourish again this barren land

Land & earth that will inhabit again all of the elements of creation

If not now then when will you surrender?

## Home

Let us build a home

Like the home the bird makes for its future family and children

High up in the tree

Simply out of sticks and leaves

A home that lasts and withstands the challenging realities of this

beautiful world and its seasons


The many flavors of this life'


A home that lasts

before we fly away

I hold in my hands what keeps us

What keeps us apart?

Apart for eternity

innocence

## Amorphous

You enter and leave this world through the element of

Earth and fire

Evolution and desolation intertwined

Entangled in this world

For some time and space

Transforming and gone

Yet remaining in the scattered remains

In between form and amorphous

**Paradox**

The paradox of being told you are free

While living in a country that has always oppressed you for the

color of your skin

That and much more


But words don't do justice

Nothing actually seems to bring justice in a world that is naturally

beautiful but has societally been made unjust by power hungry,

nature destroying conflicted humans


Free

Well injustice is the only element that truly

roams freely


People forget history when it is convenient or simply out of pure

ignorance

Who thought ignorance could be pure?

But not knowing at least gives you an opportunity to learn

Who could have imagined their innocence attacked simply for

existing?

Life always gives us the ability to learn

innocence

My deepest respect and reverence

Eternally for a people and community that accepted me

Open in allowing one to take space and express presence

Even If it wasn't completely and it was complex

It was indeed the closest I had known to perfection

Perfection of simply existing and expressing presence

Now most of the world takes from this beautiful acceptance but seems to have been born blind to the responsibility of healing the collective suffering

Give back as well
Don't just take

Remember the origins
Remember the people
Remember their years of suffering
Remember their years of joy regardless of the circumstance

The same joy you were able to cherish within your existence
Solidarity without justice is like the absence of the unity between my body and my breath in this lifetime

Without end

innocence

Let the injustice come to an end my people

All my people you are


Listen to those oppressed voices

Listen to the Black screams for peace, justice and equality

Don't let the innocence die

Don't let the silent screams fall on deaf ears

Even if you can't see or hear


Let this innocence live

With all of my life

Let this innocence live


The innocence will always return time and time again

In every time and space

For eons

What you and others share is silence

The common language

innocence

The unknown force

Surrender

Millenniums will pass

Yet our minds

Still wont understand

Surrender

Perhaps a form beyond questions and answers

will arrive

It is what it is


It is meant to be the way it is

And it is by chance


All simultaneously perhaps

**In** _____**between**

Leaving and staying

Life and death

Absence and presence

In between

innocence

Passion is beyond expectation

Or for purpose

Intense exuberance of emotions

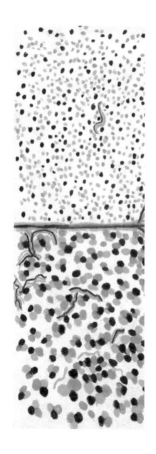

innocence

Submitting to The distance

No it doesn't

scare me

Well maybe a little


We never part ways

If we are forever connected

Dwelling in the moment

One forgets to leave


Beauty for the mystics is chaos for the pragmatics of this world

**Oblivious to the oblivion**

Floating and romancing the mysteries of

The unknown

Roaming with the sensations

What is the matter if it's a paradox?

Roam until you reach a point

Beyond exploration

or fulfillment

The boundless encapsulated outside of the bounded

Exploring inward

clarity of what is felt

Oblivion continues to grow until it

never grew

Depth is always present,

you just have to notice It

A present waiting to be

revealed to the unseen

Residing no where

and simultaneously

in the past, future

and present

innocence

We must all go

one day

or

one night

But are we really

departing, escaping

or

just continuing

the journey

from where we

are at

right now

innocence

The realm of secrets and lies can be treacherous

A land sinking with every step you can't fathom

Worlds shattered before words are even uttered

When and where did the lie start and the truth become an illusion

visited once in a while?

The new dies before its presence can even be mourned

The beauty of poetry

is not in recital

or performance


It comes

as it

goes

innocence

## A room – The room – the home

A room is magical

It can protect you from the outside

At the same time

Showing you yourself

The world

And your world


The first place traveled

without stepping

in or out


This time and space

You have been allocated


Perhaps under conditions that you will find a way to destroy

with the freedom you found from what others

may see as an imprisonment

A box


Liberation to go where you want

Now


And do so how you want to

Thank you

I wasn't able to fully say it then

Human don't normally thank what they see as inanimate objects

But thank you

Thank you for taking care of me

Drifting for days

The tide between

Night and day

Diminishing


How can we sleep

Knowing we live and die?

**Surrender**

Surrender your mind for a few

You don't always need to analyze, categorize and judge

Your mind is a container that can't fill

The vastness of this life

As my words here can not

fill the mystery of the writer

simply feel the air around you

Close your eyes for a moment

Look within

and then open them

and look up

the division is gone

the sky is there

so are the clouds

and soon as the sun begins to say goodbye

The stars will also come to play

perhaps even the moon

Let your mind be like this

Without layers

Yet at times appearing as a

Multitude of layers

Like the sky or Like the oceans

that reflect the endless dimensions of the sky while

also holding the uncharted depths within

**Found & Lost**

Lost myself

Then found you


What it felt like to lose

You time and time again

Feeling what was gone

And then realizing


You never left

You

I

The younger innocent

Me

You were still here

The innocence

before the pain

**You - Who?**

I met others but seemed to forget you

Perhaps not in whole

But in pieces?

It is crazy and utterly fascinating to perceive that this

body will drop one day into the infinite depths of this world.

Yet how much time have we spent

Time with just ourselves?

The uncharted depths most will never understand

What does it mean to love oneself

To spent time with yourself

Just you

Just

you

It is through ourselves that we come to let the heart flow

Like the water in our bodies connecting to the water of the vast

Seas we live on in this world

The power of nature

Unfelt

Feel the immensity

Let the intuition of the heart free from the chambers of your mind

and the minds of conformity

Silence

The language of all existence

The mysterious beauty

The answers to the questions

The questions to the answers


Even in the songs the birds sing

There is

Silence

Force & flow

Two rhythms within

Everywhere

## The longing for peace

The longing for peace lays dormant like the

Snake on the jungle floors

Hidden

Mysterious yet

Waiting to be seen

To be felt

To be activated forever and now

There is no dead end to this journey

The journey to the beyond

The endless journey without an end

The path comes to be revealed with

Time and space

## Sold out & in

You have sold out to the colonizers and their tongue

No longer do you remember what your ancestors protected for so long

Yes there is evolution that is needed within the culture and history of

every people but you live not in alignment of the ancestors


But instead in the same systems, world, rhetoric and ideology that was

forcefully imposed on our people

Where is the justice for the ancestors when you chose to inflict yourself

with choosing this poison and living in oblivion to the medicine that

lasted thousands of years and still does in many pockets of this world?

Do not forget

Do not give them any more power

They have fooled all of us people of color, people of the land for far

too long

There has never been a time to be silent

But there has also never been a time to continue following the colonial

remnants of a historical past that continues to perpetuate the injustices

of the past.

Our potentials of bringing about a world that once was indigenous and

free from the violence of the colonizers now resides in the hearts,

minds, bodies and souls of those alive in this time onwards.

innocence

Who will sleep to the silent screams of the ancestors?

Who will restore honor and righteousness to that which was taken and

continuously taken?

When will the innocence be restored

In a world occupied by tyrants the innocence shall return

Hear me through these silent words

The innocence is back

because it never left

How can I forget you

O creator

You who has been here all along

Beyond form yet with form

For countless eons

And remaining so without end

My longing fulfilled with the taste of your

Nectar

Tell me my creator

The divine

How can I surrender myself in every way possible to you?

I desire nothing but this

Tell me and I will do it

Every way possible until my last breath and beyond


I will give my entire being in your embrace

I know now

As I must have known before that this longing is connected to you

The end and beginning of me

Is you

Only you


Tell me O Creator

How may I surrender myself in a way that all of me is yours forever?

That look

Long ago

Spoke it all

Just because it is not tangible

doesn't mean it is not accessible

Unmeasurable energy comes from the dark unexplored areas of existence.

Even in our own individual existences and the pain and suffering they may contain.

Not dark meaning negative but dark as in a realm beyond expectations and perceptions.


Doesn't need to make sense

Where did we come from?

Where do we return

No answers needed

Connecting to the self

Feel like I haven't been selfish for a long while

Not selfish like lost in the self

More like just spending quality time with your first friend - you

That's all

Exploring

You find the old in the new and the new in the old

The discovery of this world is endless

Even if our days were endless

Our search would remain

Endless


Dead ends don't exist

The endless beginnings do


What is the end but a beginning to the end

Gratitude to creation

For every step my feet take

On this earth


How so many lose remembrance of this gift


The gift of gratitude

The feeling

of when we first discover facets of the world

from tapping into the joy and raw curiosity hidden

in exploration

**Coming as we go**

We came into each other's lives

Like the unknown

A breeze as subtle as the dawn of

A new day

Yet

The wind as abrupt and gushing as the one that hovers over the

Himalayan mountains

Your beauty fills my eyes with tears

Never together

But sometimes

Many times

We cry alone

The clouds containing our heavy longing burst open the power of

The monsoon

Outside of our bodies our essence floats

Here together at last

Where do we go

When home is everywhere?


June 19 2006

Part words like waves

My lips speak silence

Where do you start and where do I end?

innocence

Hey you

Yes you

You living in your mind

When are you gonna come out here and play?

innocence

Sometimes

The path is to be walked alone

.

innocence

I need change

Connect with yourself

all while somehow

Helping those that are starving physically, mentally, emotionally and
spiritually

reach self-realizations

Just by simply connecting with yourself

Here for a moment

I drift

Flowing away with my breath

From and to the dark light

That found me

Together

The spirit and soul roam

Asking me to come home

On this path often

I walk alone

That which is not

The presence and absence of the being

Long cold

Winter nights

Alone

Uncharted depths of the unknown

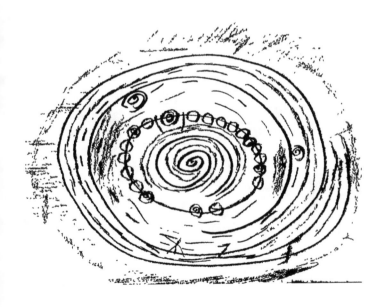

innocence

A bit of mind

A lot of heart and spirit


Is life an experience of remembering and forgetting?

Take me

All that clothes me

Is yours

For you

My divine

Until I can't see in the

Darkness of the night

Blinded by your light

Take me

The body adorned or naked

I surrender

To you

The endless

Touch a tree

The way you would embrace

A new born

Their healing capacity beyond life and death

Gave up my will to live

For a collection of moments

Seemed to have lasted for years

Redeemed

Exuberance for life


Flying high and free like a kite

No strings attached

Released

Uniting instead with the invisible

Strands of life

Keeping it close to me

But not closed from release


Fine

I know I am

Fine

But what am I?

What was eternal and timeless

Remained so

The magic never left

It shaped forms

Different yet similar as before

Cry

Do not harden

Your strength is in many forms

Not just in holding it together

Don't hold it in

What is sin but a taboo?

The world tells you to toughen up

To forget

Feel

My brother

Feel

My sister

Feel

All along

Along the way

You were looking

For yourself

Looking for a way within

Where you could sit and see

Where you could feel and just be

Standing

In my home or house for some time

Every single way and day

Sunlight moonlight

Shadows and all

Light peaking through

Dark dripping and slipping like dears in the spaces

That used to be home

Without fears

Lost in the forest of our minds

What is time beyond our mind?

What is beyond but to be?

To belong to look beyond

Why look?

Seeking

Seeking to never find

Just seek

## AwakenTheYouth

AwakenTheYouth is a project I started back in 2011.

It is time to revitalize the original mission of bringing awareness of how the youth benefits from lightness and guidance in their lives. There were few but still there were some people in my life, perhaps by chance that allowed me to awaken my abilities and potentials stored deep within me at 16-17 years old. They didn't catalyze this awakening I did. However they did leave an impression on me of difference between them and other humans I encountered; there was a difference, one of positive value.

Ultimately I changed my life and my perspectives on life from navigating my own depth. I had years of built in resentment for those that could have reached out and made an impact on my life by simply showing compassion but they didn't. I had to learn on my own and be my own teacher. Like I said there were a few in my life but only I that could elevate myself from the depths I drowned in unconsciously or consciously.

My mission isn't to be teacher in the public school system, it used to be. I used to crave to be a high school history teacher. Shit I went to a university or it, got a degree and then realized the failures of the system. There was a tremendous amount of passion for this; in high school after the tenth grade when I had my mental, emotional, spiritual and physical awakening I spent more time with teachers than students. This was because I saw them as the vehicles of change in the lives of us as students and I wanted to learn not just the subject they taught but everything they knew. The teachers had an overwhelming power that even they didn't fully understand.

I would later learn that their stifled passion and awareness was because of bureaucracy, political, financial and social structures outside of their control. Just like medical professionals or other professionals, some of these teachers genuinely wanted to help us as students and to teach us critical thinking skills. Unfortunately their original passion for getting into their professions was obliterated by the structural suffocations mentioned above. However, I also energetically could differentiate between the teachers that had this passion even if it wasn't expressed to us as students and the ones that truly were not

innocence

aware or didn't care.

I've learned that critical thinking skills are not taught but even if they were they would not be enough on their own. Teaching emotional intellegience, coping and skills to feel emotions safely are vital for the true evolution of a human being and thus of a student. It would make sense to draw the connection between being a human being and being a student since learning is what differentiates us as extensions of life or organisms. But what can we learn from teachers and people that don't have any emotional intelligence to feel their own emotions or that of their students that are forced to be taught in concrete square or rectangular prisons with rigid doors, walls, ceilings, décor and execution styled chairs?

Instead of suffocating in structures that seemed the destiny of a teacher in this society I instead invested in myself again, again and again. The ancestral knowledge of yoga taught me how to cope, release and understand my repressed emotions and thoughts.

Since then with this knowledge I have taught in juvenile detention centers, refugee camps, group homes, public and private schools and various other spaces. One constant lesson I have learned

innocence

regardless of the time period or the space that I had these experiences in is that most of the personnel within these spaces are not emotionally connected to themselves and the system they operate in or simply put are employed by. They do not care to breed connections that lead to the healing of oneself. So how can you heal others when you don't know how to heal yourself or when you are not allowed to because of the bureaucracy? Everything mentioned above is centered on healing, growth and transformation and the commonality between them all is connection.

The teachers, institutions, personnel, spaces and times that always have and will continue for eons to have the most impact are the ones that give us space to exist, understand us and what is understanding but a word that really means emotional connection? It is a responsibility to foster emotional connections that lead to the depth hidden within all of us; not a choice but an inherent responsibility. Individual healing leads to collective healing and individual consciousness leading to collective consciousness.

I am only human I will die one day as will everyone but I

innocence

don't want others to suffer as I did and perhaps by chance stumble upon

this inner knowing. Instead I want and need every human that reads this

to know there is beauty in everything that is you.

Change is needed and I know that change will come through the feeling

process.

**Is education creating ignorance of nature & natural living?**

How many children and "adults" that used to be children still go outside and spend time in nature?

Climb trees

Swim

Run

Walk

Sit

Sleep

movement or stillness

Outside in this beautiful nature that we have been born into

Our first home not house

Don't be chained to what you thought you were taught or educated

Those ignorant to the ways of nature are not qualified to be teachers yet alone students.

The inherent imprisonment within the introduction of that conditioning needs to be thrown away not recycled for even another moment.

Drifting

Sometimes drifting

I am a collection of leaves

Floating with the breeze

The roots of my being resembling a

1000 year old tree

Eternity

In those moments

My heart strops

The guard drops

Layers of locks freed open

The universe has delivered the key

I am here

Do you feel?

Do you see?

Emotions that were sealed away

Now today

They release

A piece of the process of peace

Begins

An end to the cycle

Embarking on a journey to the oasis

Of my heart

There is no mission

No objective

The distance closes

Roaming

Seeking to simply seek

The mysterious beauty of life and death

For they are one

The unity of the Divine masculine & Divine feminine

The stars and the soil

With no beginning or end

**What about…?**

What about all those lives

Those begging on the curb that are now gone

Those searching in trash cans for food?

Confused for insolence

They look up at you

Thinking it could be their auspicious day to receive an offering

Yet empathy lost and distorted

Where is the compassion?

When did we as human beings begin to lose value for another human's

suffering?

Societal suffering and personal suffering

The layers of suffering present simultaneously

You see a human being begging or searching for a way out

But have you ever wondered from what or where this begging or

searching is coming from?

Or is comfort for one's life in capitalism enough to satisfy our full

stomachs while the hearts and consciousness starve?

Who will remember them

Or are they forgotten for eternity?

Lost with the wind

While we continue to walk or drive by

innocence

Lets talk identity and its complexities

First generation American

Son of an immigrant

Punjabi household

Raised and born in the southside of Richmond


Of the many

only a few I give access to here


Don't ever assume you know

You don't know shit

Moments frozen

The constant of change

will be challenged

In these frozen moments

Do something you love continuously without end for a

few hours, days or years

Let this flow state grow

Lay down for a moment

Close your eyes

Feel your emotions

Drift in your imagination

Screens are not the only subjects of perception that require unbroken

concentration.

**The laze**

The truth within the poetic state

The laze

The laze that reveals the unfathomable

depth

There is nothing productive about avoiding peace of presence

To just sit or lay or stand or float

Without care

Who is to judge this and why?

Must we do something to become something

or is there a balance between

drifting in this indolence and

activating the relentless passion for this life?

Why do something when you can do nothing and be everything

This life that is still like the trees with hidden roots as old as the earth

that they reside in

Fluid and tumultuous as the rip currents of the ocean

Breezy as the transitional wind between spring and summer and

summer and fall

Let us sway and stay here for a bit

Perhaps never again

My tears will never wash you away

From my memory

From my heart

From my body

You are the unknown


You always have been

You always will be


You who will always be

Perhaps life & death meet where the consciousness perceives itself

innocence

What is

within the sands of time and space

will reveal itself

in the fathomless depths


The unknown

# Chapter 2
# Pain & Suffering

Reside in this pain with me

Let me take you to a

space & time

Inescapable to the human experience

The heart floating and

drowning in chaos

simultaneously

Do not downplay your

Pain

Embrace it

Suffering isn't always eternal

Meet and greet this pain in the same way you choose avoidance

Who knows what will happen

We created it

I tried to bring it back and hold it

Together

Us

You destroyed it

I finally accepted

innocence

How hard it is to trust

innocence

Innocence

The young boy

The young girl

kidnapped and taken

away from their family

How can it be?

Lives that were once free

now sold into

human trafficking

modern type of slavery

the many modern types

Look at the bravery of these children

the pain continues to kill them

yet they continue to endure

forcefully made to explore

ways of living

hard to even imagine

taking the childhood innocence

instead of giving them the beauty of freedom

The beauty of freedom

Treated like nothing

Sold and manipulated for a monetary sum

Enjoyed by sickly twisted people

Addicts not held responsible for their habits

Some of these children live on by maintaining hope

While others choose or chose to leave this world

By the rope

Still there are others who choke

All that remains is the blood from the scars that were never soaked

Continuing to become prone to provoking oneself to choke away in

silence

In a state of depression because of the violence and the physical,

mental, emotional and spiritual violation

Mutilation of a human life

The children left to slowly suffer

The pain from being continuously stabbed by a knife

Is it right that a human life

has no right

To its own life?


The children close their eyes hoping to fly away into the sky

To finally soar freely

Instead of being treated like an animal slaved away into a dark cage

Fills me with rage

to recognize children of every age

are distorted to made to think of

life as a nothing but a maze

a maze that has no exit

the pain and torture

left its stain on the remains

passing the defense mechanisms to become engrained permanently in

every reach of the brain

you tell me

Would living like this not make you insane?

Insane insaan

Tears falling like the monsoon rain

Realize that life for these kids does not have to be this way

Break the chain that maintains the enslavement

Stand up for their rights and make a change

PLEASE MAKE A CHANGE

## Wishes

My death wish is no surprise clue

Fuck karma I face trauma daily and optimism never fails me but

today my key to the happiness has self-destructed

Fuck it – death waiting to be constructed

So like I said birth days be the worst days

Death

O how I may get a taste

forever

"This is my death letter"

**Farmer suicides in Punjab**

Who hears their silent screams

Who perceives their cremated dreams

1947

1970

1984 Genocide

2012

2020

Time and space create change but not here

Who feels the nightmares they lived and buried themselves with until

the last resort of death itself?

Questions are endless

Answers to the uncertain plight of those that feed the stomachs of

countless humans that don't even know where their food comes from

are still lost in the abyss of bureaucracy.

Let's talk identity and its complexities

First generation American

Son of an immigrant

Punjabi household

Raised and born in the southside of Richmond

Of the many only a few I give access to here

Don't ever assume you know

You don't know shit

innocence

Bring peace to those who cannot speak

Justice to those who cannot or could not

(if they no longer remain here in the physical)


Feel, think or breath because silent screams

Have desolated the beautiful dream that could have been


Don't let them continue to

silently scream


Please don't let them continue to

Silently scream

innocence

The customs and beliefs of the indigenous and non-white people

destroyed and buried

Is life not for everyone to live in their own way?

It is not right for a human to not have a say on one's own life.

Now I have finally deciphered the scheme

Finally able to see the world for what it is

Not taking it entirely for what it seems

Realizing I don't have to work all day and night to accumulate cream

Instead I live on

To fulfill my dream of

peace

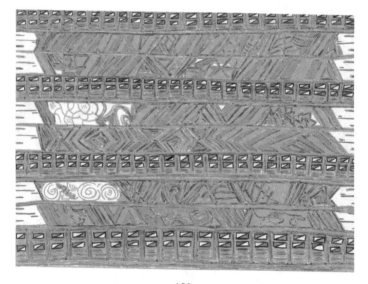

How can I Forgive and forget?

Will I forgive and forget?

### Recounted Justice /Justice Recounted

To the white man, a representative of an organization who lied, violated the trust I entrusted and who didn't see my value as a practitioner and more importantly a human being that wanted to share from his heart in utter devotion to selfless service at a suicide walk. Why? Just because I didn't have a title to offer to you and your organization? What if this was my outlet to staying in this world? The blood and loss of life would be on your hands! How many like me have you letdown?!

American Foundation for Suicide Prevention, what a cruel joke.

I forgive.

But never shall I forget how you don't walk with truth; how you are a puppet of ignorance and status. For many that came that day in remembrance or in current moments of uncertainty, you have buried them alive in their surrender of innocence and sensitivity. You violate not honor the earth below your desolating feet. The sacred violated in a world within a world of people suffering from memories of losing those no longer in this world. Injustice personified; you don't know how to honor and hold sacred space, your dollar shall not go far.

You are not a leader, you don't get it, fuck your titles. You are the origin point of the same lack of understanding, judgement, despair and uncertainty that led one and many others that walked toward the exit of this reality. There is a difference between suffering of the self and societal suffering. As you read this others also walk this path regardless of whether you read this yesterday, read it today or will see these words in the future.

Not all life is left behind because of pain; some go of free will.
No one can judge because what is wrong and what is right?

Tell me white man!

Since you are the authority apparently.

You who violate the beauty of those living, tell me who are you to tell me about the decisions of the dead!

Indeed in fact through many feel pushed to go, and who can blame them to go away from a world of humans that lie and hide within the illusions that they have created?

The illusions that now have become the artificial light; the sun kept in the hollows of the unknown.
Not to worry
Your fake gestures and worries are not a necessity now
The shadows will get a voice
O my fellow humans
The voice will come

**Where is the justice**

Where is the justice?

This is just it

The true nature of the practice and application of equality

No solidarity with the truth

What good was your so called morality ?

Good people misused for the singular purpose of profit

Fuse the passion with the fire of caring and compassion

The task is to dream into existence a world filled with justice and not

leaving the world as it just is

everywhere I look I see injustice

Hiding and show casing a grim stare

No I don't and won't keep silent

Everything I say is for the people

Who can't speak

Who can't hear

Who can't openly seek justice due to the fear that exists here

Maybe if I stand up for what is every human's birth right others will be

inspired to join in the ongoing freedom struggle and fight

Living in injustice is a shock

Surrounded and strangled in a world that has no key for the lock

innocence

Not being able to talk or

peacefully meditate and walk

because of the thoughts that rot my brain

due to the twisted knot

that injustice has created

freedom that has been traded

humanity seems to have faded and evicted from reality


But freedom is an opportunity that still awaits

We just need to take action after

connection

**Listen**

Tears flow down her eyes but no one is there to listen

Silent hissing by the perpetrator raping and viciously molesting the

young girl or boy

with kisses

A human life is worth more than a diamond pearl

But chaos is the only thing that swirls around here

That and fear

Shaking the girl to the ground

The coward continues in the background

Look around and listen and you will not feel

you will not hear the silent screams

The sounds are no where to be found

but inside the girl or boy

the young girl and boy who could have smiled

who could have laughed

who could have been warmly embraced yet she and he are dead

It may not appear so from the outside but

within they are hurting to the core

nothing left to explore but

silence

who gave others the permission to take a life away before it could be

lived?


Give me answers to that question if you can

and if you can't then take this as a lesson

Live everyday with the passion

The inner blessing from embracing truth to bring justice


to those who can't speak

Justice

to those who can not feel

think

or breathe because silent screams have

drowned and desolated the beautiful dreams that could have been


O what could have been

Don't let them continue to silently scream


Please don't let them continue to silently scream

**Child Molestation**

Test him Test her

Treated like a lab rat

or another sort of animal

violating another human seems to be their motive

no remorse

taking a child's innocence and happiness by force

a human life fiddled with like an experiment and left riddled with layers

of trauma

What is the hypothesis?

Destroying a human's self worth seems to be the plan

The perpetrators continue committing injustice in clear sight

Blind eyes

What is the point of rule of law when no justice is enforced in the dark

corners of this society?

Pain from molesting occurs every moment

again and again

How can you carry out this crime for your whole life span?


The children ran

The children sang

They played and enjoyed

Now they are manipulated

Pain and sorrow replacing the past joys

Giving light on a topic rarely discussed

Without hesitation

I won't spare

I won't care to end your life

if in this violation you are complicit

Serving justice so that you may never take another human being's

integrity

I won't just let it be and I hope those listening will also not let it be.

-18 year old self speaking

Taking time to give my devotion, passion and love to this strength

This wisdom that resides within

innocence

I pour everything

nothing stings

does your heart ring

for me

like the way your phone

rang all the

nights I desperately

hit the call button


I felt so hurt

So tough to

give everything and


for it still not be

enough

**Together**

We grew up together

You and I

Regardless of whether

Bibi was not here anymore

Or if Paapa was

You and I

Exploring our youth

as children

Flowing along with patterns but

also breaking them

Fighting yet also making up

Exploring new depths new paths

regardless if Momi

came home finally

what felt like finally

But socially was 5:30pm

give or take

with food

for our little stomachs

some warmth for our hearts

nourishment of everything is important right?

Or whether it was

Daddi

arriving to the house

I mean home

late at night

O how the time passed and passes

Then and today

We explored yet still the voyage of growing up continues

Growing up from seeds to fully fledged plants blooming

in the spring

Sometimes appearing to be in the cycles of winter

The end – the regrowth

The destruction of the old

O how we grew up together

Separated for a few

but not forever

But now

because there is nothing but now

Now without the past, the grudges, the anger, the pain, the frustrations

Now

Shall we move forward

and grow up together some more?

I would like to

How about you?

innocence

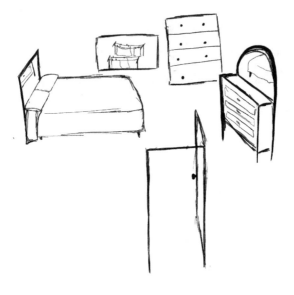

Time heals

Every night is a new day

my grandmother

the moments I spent with you

I witnessed your resilience

even as you sat on your death bed

pace maker

dying away little by little

day by day

as I laid my bed next to her bed

taking care of her

in the room

that I would later receive and reside in

for 17 years

innocence

Emotions are not weak

They don't make you weak

I want to say this

Even if I am not here

One day


I want others to always know this

The beauty of emotions

Roaches in the house

The struggles

To get here

My own

My father's

My mother's

My grandmother's

My grandfather's

My sister's

My brother's

My ancestor's

Struggle and sacrifice

**Surrender**

No fear of any man or death

Fear itself brings about the realization of your truth if you can see past

the fear.

It is better to lose your head than your essence.

Don't be scarred

This is when and where you stand up and put your power into your

presence.

Let that neutral energy remain dormant in your eyes, hands and feet

until the time to reveal has come.

In that moment let it come from peace not malice.

But remember to never

Never

Surrender to anyone but the divine

Memories

People

The connections

Remembered and scattered

In time frames

Unaware

Of how important their entire existence is to me


How hard it is for me to

Trust again

To let myself fully

feel again

## Killer

Peace and compassion are essential yet destruction of what is dead is beautiful.

Let us focus on prisons where there is no rehabilitation present however there are lies present that state that the construct and foundation of the design serves that purpose. The only purpose is to enslave black bodies and people of color here in the USA and every other country that has inherited the post colonialist and imperialistic constructs. The design is not rehabilitation but destruction of the will and freedom to live. This is no different than public schools that claim education as the main reason for its existence yet in reality indoctrination to systems of oppression are the real motive. There is no peace and never will there be in power manipulative societies that lock up human beings in a cage and treat them like animal. This is utterly inhumane! Where and how will peace exist where there exists the injustices of letting others roam freely just because of their social or economic clearance or the color of their white skin and the privilege that comes with it? Who are the real killers?
 Who are the real criminals?

What I understand is that authorities can walk around with pistols on their hips and badges on their chest and thus are given free jurisdiction and permission to end my life and I can't do anything about it? Lapdogs of a racist, exploitive, post-colonialist and post

innocence

imperialist system. Fuck that I come from an ancestry of warriors. If my peace is disturbed by these cowards that hide behind badges, titles and bureaucracies then it is my birth right to return ruthless.

Take the rules away and let us see what this society looks like! Even though the rules in this current society don't apply to you if you are white because your tribe is the honorary exemption in this world. An exemption that conscious and unconscious beings allow for what reason? This can no longer exist because there will be no increase in collective consciousness until every life and specifically black lives are given the same freedom and privilege that a white life has had in the contemporary and the historical record. Remnants of colonialism, racism and imperialism have to be destroyed while patriarchy still waits to be challenged and addressed.

It is beautiful to destroy that which has caused harm and is now yearning to be dead.

Indigenous roots of reciprocity will remind us of the beauty of what was before our ancestors were slain by these people and their ideologies. It is time to destroy and look within.

The stigma of being a killer somehow doesn't exist for those that have been granted what seems like an eternal invitation to slaughter in these white made systems of oppression.

Peace has been disturbed and now it is time for rejuvenation to return at last.

innocence

**Leech**

Life is a long process or it can be depending on your decisions.

Listen

There are very few so called friends but many leeches.

How many are gonna stay down for the count when you need them?

Cut off more than half your fingers and then add up the number remaining.

Most are snakes just looking for an opportunity to come up.

Opportunists feeding off of your energy.

Like as if you didn't work and grind day and night for what previously was not tangible. Sometimes you can't even get to the grind because the association to these leeches throws you into a pattern of chaos and turmoil.

There will be a few friends

A few real friends that will go to death and back for you. Those reading these words know who they are. But otherwise stay in tune with your intuition and innocence because it will tell you the truth even where illusions are present.

Don't ever be anyone that you are not. Stay true to your identity and all its intricacies because you shouldn't have to limit your life expressions for anyone.

If they walk away when you need them then close the access previously given.

It may seem like a sacrifice but it is an investment into yourself.
Keep your head lifted in confidence and optimism but also profoundly humble.

Don't wait on transformation instead hustle for it.

Let your eyes be pierced from the focus and dedication but soft from compassion.

Wake up

Your greatness is waiting.

The friend that just disappeared

Without a word

Without a trace

The sadness that exists inside for a

time unknown

In an instance

I thought I forgot

I thought I moved past


But then in an instance

The feelings of you

are back


All the pain, all of the acceptance

of what can not be and will never be

In this life

for us – all the ifs

yet with a smile

I embrace this heart wrenching longing

Open arms – come


I surrender my heart to you

In life and death

How can I say

I like you

When I don't know

Who you are?

innocence

**"Crazy"**

Crazy but one day maybe

My insane thoughts will become lazy

Reality seems pointless

Missing the point but not resulting to the joint

Made a commitment about

5 years ago

to forever say no to any mind-altering substance

But I realized recently use doesn't mean abuse

and that it is not mind altering because when does anything in life not

alter in the vortex of change?

Change in other words meaning life.

Yet I chose to take this pain

without the anesthesia

progress doesn't mean gain

without love simple existence is impossible

yet nothing else is possible in the end anyways

**Mine**

These words

These words that I felt

when you chose to leave

Even when my devotion, passion and love stood testament of our love

I will never get to call you mine

Will I

In this life?

Never will I feel the comfort and warmth of your presence in the cold

winters of this world.

Alone never together

That is what we are to each other

Will memory of me soon fade from your mind?

Will someone else begin to preoccupy your time?

Perhaps you heart and mind as well

Will the mystery of life wash away the moments that we once shared?

The utter sweetness

Of union

As impartial as perhaps

Its blossoming will ever be

Don't forget

Don't let me go

Please


Everything changes like the wind in this world

You will grow


But never will I forget you or our love

Some people change

Forgetting the moments that will never be again


Are you one to change and forget?

A loss beyond grief

**Lost**

My life goal has been to help others

But I am lost

So how can I help my sisters and brothers when I am unstable?

My life seems to be a fable

That has no meaning

Existing as a human being without feeling

Eyes open and mind on

But feels like the system is going through sabotage and shutdowns

Smiles turn into frowns

## Silence – Part 1 & Part 2

The silent screams continues

Hoping that when the eyes close

I will have beautiful dreams

But to the opposite

Only nightmares arise


In silence the pain further develops

They won't sense it

How would they know if I'm fine?

They don't spare the time or dare to find the truth of the person before

their eyes

and so the chance

slips – the final glance

The silent dreams

eclipsed now by the totality of silence


The same silence which started to end any sort of timeline of peace

Now has instilled tranquility

Instead of numbing any of the emotions

The intensity of each and every emotion is embraced

Transported to the well within

Discovering the hidden water within

Quenching the longing for stability and the submerged depth

Every molecule of this body

now floating in the humility of the reservoir discovered while drowning

183

innocence

In the past

The support was gone

Perhaps never present

Surely never felt or experienced

I am supposed to surrender and trust others?

Most would see this as an excuse

But that is not the truth

Sometimes we avoid the lows

So we get high to get by

Soul serving as wings

I begin to fly

Your pain is real

Let it out and cry

No reason to hide

Why remain in limbo and lie?

Confide in your confidence versus your pride


Freedom has to be chosen

Something you can never

buy


Life is a beautiful journey

Enjoy the ride

Some things you let die and

Wither away

Instead of giving life

Love isn't one of them

After all of it

Do you think you could just come back?

Without any remembrance of the loss given

That there would be a place for you in this smothered soul


Where would you return to look for me?

An adolescent's dreams coming true after years of confusion, pain and void.

Consistency, resilience and clarity creating the vision for these dreams.

I kept faith in myself, even when no one else did.

It got me here

innocence

Healing is healing

My healing is mine but also yours

Our healing is everyone's healing

Let this be a space of healing

Immovable is the body when forged with the will

Of the mind and spirit of the soul

innocence

Sometimes we all just need a reminder

That we are not alone

Not far away

But in fact

We are close

We are one.

Inspiration creates motivation

Everything in life flows

Overcoming trauma through yoga and art

Reclaiming the body and mind

Moments turnt into dayz

of reflecting

and thinking of you

The difficulty of having let go but still feeling the need

Lingering on the sensations

Heart steady

Sometimes most times racing

Even though pain emerges

On the surface and deep in the interior

**Many times**

Many times in my mind

I find the piece of peace

Laying scattered and distorted

Clarity I am not seeing or feeling

Physically distant I'm becoming

not running

Leaving it all behind

But carrying remnants of the dark depth of the past

Pulsating my heart

Until the beat

Skips a beat

All forms of physicality become affected

The bones severed due to the places of my being neglected

Clarity never again

Choosing to step into this

This space

This endless flow yet chase

Memories of my grandmother

Remembering being a witness to the soul's departure

Or of initiating the cremation of the body into ashes of my maternal

grandfather

The scared body scattered in ashes of ether

Yet the spirit remains

The knowledge was always engrained

Just needed to be tapped into

Reflected back into the prism of my life

The endless hues of the colors

Drowning in this depth

Can't float when merging becomes impossible

Surrendering in countless ways

Moments turned and passed into days

Into months

Into years

Tears struck from the loosening grip of the dark unknown

The dark unknown

Fear

Screams released

Silent screams

In the twilight

The journey of returning

Whether it may ever be completed

Some things stay in the unmanifest

Realms

Never to be touched yet never to be forgotten

The immense power piercing every layer

Every boundary

Until everything collapses

This spirit and soul releases from the release of the body

Floating along

Drifting away


Away and here is a matter of distance

Matter

The physical space and time

Transcending and surrendering simultaneously

**Waiting**

I waited

In the desert

Longing for the oasis

But there was a drought

One day

Clouds gathered

And it finally rained

A storm came and left

Taking away the pain

The destruction remained

Magic appeared

The seeds began to grow

Growth of the winter in the spring

Sprung in the winter

**The pain remained......**

Shackling me outside the body as I

Felt the chaos consume from within

How did it pass?

Did it pass or did I move?

Or get moved?

Like a cage made out of raw iron

I made it to keep you out

No more pain

Not this time


What had so much warmth

Now desolate

Now so cold

It was the heart first

But the eyez spoke the narrative

Never again

Lost in the daze

Lost in the vortex

Never again

Or as i say

My heart is my bed

There I lay
Next to the streams

The secrets eventually came out

On that couch

In that room

Tilted back

Looking at the ceiling and walls

Waiting in vain

**Struggles and pain**

Who do I share this with?

Who cares

To know the depth

Or dares to link the energies with magic

Longing to blend

Blending in union with the streams

Suspend the lines of reality and dreams

Moments of drifting

Slipping into a space

A dimension without trace

No return back to bodily existence

Will you miss me?

To see to be free

No one cares to feel

To peal the layers of depth

Many think they know me

But do they?

Everyone chooses the fake over the real

The illusion over the truth

But who cares right?

Wrong

innocence

## Coping

How does one cope?

What are the methods?

How we cope with life consciously or unconsciously affects our reality

profoundly.

Many make the grave decision to step on the gentleness of how others

cope.

Even that is coped with somehow


Question yourself


How do I cope?

Every day

Every day pain

Drove me sane

The scar seems to always heal

The layers seem to never peal

Zoning in a dark room

Finding a fragment

Piece of peace

Release this pain I shall

Absorb every part of my being into molecules

No rules to existence

Awakening peace and prosperity

That night there

In that dark beautiful space

It was coming to an end

The pain wouldn't mend

the scars


Soon I'm far away

Guiding the breath out of my being

Feeling the essence


Ready to let go of this existence

No need to remain

Yes I am sane


Leaving the physicality isn't insanity


Who will be open to understanding this with compassion instead of

judgement?

innocence

**Restoration of energy**

Connection to the breath

Separation of energies

The breath reveals how to prepare and receive

Restore

The sounds are simplistic

Yet profound

Do you hear the rhythm of what was lost?

What if you leave?

I know it will be alright

But what if I desired to explore more

What if I don't just want to be alright?


Insane with no one to hear

The fear

That was here and everywhere

The silent screams

Dried up tears

Surrendered and forgotten dreamz


Inside


I feel this melody inside


Healing the depths of pain

## Once shook

Reeling in the soliloquy of time and space

The resonance of being lost yet found

The energy scattered yet coalescing

Releasing moments of sane insanity


To feel that once

Not too long ago

I almost lost the grip

Almost

Losing this body

This spark in my eyes

Almost

The magic in the vibrations of my voice


Almost letting go of the unity with my breath

But I am here

At peace with the fear

The darkness is now the light

The chaos and uncertainty is now the stability

The tears and frowns are no longer here

The smile and laughter

A rainbow arisen on a sky that was once consumed by the repressed

clouds waiting to pour

Inside

I feel this melody inside

Healing the depths of pain

Don't end yourself

Explore it

Feel it

Give yourself space

and

time

Comprehend its complexities

Love it

Live now

Die later

**Rejoice**

Simple are these words

Rejoice to see this life as a blessing

And not a curse

Sacred practices that helped me understand the pain

That caused hurt beyond words

At times questioning my self worth

The shadows slowly lifted

The darkness brought to light

A smile

Radiance serenades

Resembling the sun and the moon

The scars engrained yet the pain no longer fetters the magic

These are the colors that form my unique hue

Energy recycled yet fresh as the morning dew

Place it on my eyes and let me feel the vibrancy of life

Settled in my being

But never will I settle again

Intuitive needs

Eavesdropping into the rhythm of the universe

Watering the seed inside the seeds

One day uniting to the breath outside the breath

Inside the body of life

I join my hands together

Seeking union

Like a leaf separated from its tree

Yearning to be connected yet free

Not needing the eyes but needing to see

What is it that I want

What is it that I want to be

Not all answers are linked to questions

Energetic transmissions transforming this vital life energy

Now I fly away

Much is broken in this house

Much has been waiting to be fixed

Many times implosions have leveled those within

Yet the playing fields still seem uneven

Now it's the vital energy of this home that is leaking

Seeking clarity from the seeds planted that would one day flower into

Peace and justice

Let this house become a home

O let this house become a home!

How to hold on in a world that is

letting go?

innocence

Money is the largest religion

All are followers

We are separate yet united in truth

Claim this existence and creation

Not our creations

innocence

**Inheritance – Naw**

You think this was inherited?

Naw

Everything was built from struggle and finesse

All those hours of suffering I endured; did you go through those trials
for me?

Naw

I opened my eyes

Put my muscle to the test

Shit

Survival didn't kill me

The innocence remained protected and it will remain so.

The promise that I made to myself I still honor and will continue to do

so even after my last breath.

A society built from lies and weakness manifested in all of the

bureaucracy will crumble.

Do you think the people in it are going to be any different?

Put me anywhere

I'm gonna thrive

Enough said

You feel like home

But I know home is gonna go away

Cuz nothing ever really stays


or does it?


Enjoying the last minutes of playful

moments

**The skin – The thorn**

A torn thorn struck deep within

the fabric of the skin

What is pain

Does it remain the same or change?

Is the thorn you or simply refuged in you?

Deep in the skin

That which is foreign and known

Deep in the skin

The essence that reveals it all

Within


Deep within the skin

**When Justice Finally.........**

There came a day when justice finally arrived

An enigma

Everyone looked around

Where? Where is it? I don't see it or feel it

Everyone said.

Baffled and confused they wandered every land and every space
searching for this thing called justice.

A girl from a distance came into the scene; this girl's name was Yula.

The meaning of Yula was strength, the soothing yet resilient kind of
strength.

Yula arrived

With her hair floating everywhere elegantly

She said to the mailman who also was searching for justice while giving
to others

"Maybe justice is a friend who you never became friends with.

Maybe you never spent time to create precious moments with this

friend. Maybe it is within you

Not outside here where you are looking.

Did you ever give this friend any gifts?"

The mailman just looked at her caught off guard with his face contorted and distorted into all kinds of shapes and forms like someone

constipated for days.

Normally nothing distracted the mailman from his search for justice but

today was different.

Running fierce like the winds of a tornado came a man with a sword

Destroying everything he saw

Everything

He pushed down the mailman while he was lost in this trance.

Then the sword swinging man ran away.

Probably swinging and destroying other things in his path; everything.

Yula ran over to the mail man "are you ok" she said with the

overwhelming flow of tears down her face that were created from this

bizarre experience.

The mailman felt her concern and her compassion

The mail man's expression relaxed now and relieved in a way

He spoke "yes I'm ok, this is normal."

Yula sat there with him just listening.

"This happens often here, people come running into your space and

time trampling your quest of seeking trying to trample your peace and

humility."The man looked at his body which was bruised heavily everywhere from the fall and said "I guess I just got used to this, I know it is not right but I don't know.

What happened to me isn't right but still what can I do? I'm just a mailman. At least I am still alive, unlike others."

Yula feeling the mailman's hues of pain and peace began to feel a mix of emotions and thoughts. Yula spoke "When is the last time you played?

Lets play!"

The mailman smiling at Yula asked "what game do you want to play?"

"I don't want to play a game, I don't like games. I just want to play to play.

But first what is your name? I am Yula."

"Hmm you don't want to play a game yet you want to play, I don't know how that works but I guess I will play! My name is Finubeeblu. Lets play!"

But then as Finubeeblu looked around Yula just disappeared

Nowwhere in sight

Finubeeblu was sad

He thought he had made a friend; a friend that would play with him and maybe help him search for justice.

Then as he was lost in this sea of emotions voyaging endlessly he

innocence

remembered what she had told him "Did you give this friend any gifts?"

Finubeeblu also laughed now at how he must have looked so full of

shock when Yula had spoke and how much strength she had!

Also, how caring and compassionate she was.

How soothing her strength of precious presence was.

The gift of healing perhaps.

Finubeeblu felt a magical feeling in that moment of moments.

A change rose and roamed inside of him; his face now was radiant like a

refreshing spring day finally arriving after the mysterious void of the

winter. Finubeeblu went on his ways in this world seeking but now

without end, void of purpose, instead with presence.

Many still call him Finubeeblu the mailman

What he now delivers is the story of Yula.

The soothing yet resilient strength.


So the tale began

Maybe this is where justice was found.

Who knows?

Maybe the sword man that now sat near the ocean dwelling knows.


Floating

No longer drowning.

**The girl**

Somewhere close and known yet far away and distant.

Some called her Supna, the never ending dream.

This girl had the brightest of spirits!

When she came into this world her parents were filled with joy!

Why would they not be?

In their hands they held what had come from the divine; a blessing most powerful.

A gift

Wrapped in this gift was unique joy unparalleled.

Delight that the world had not seen nor felt.

A heart with multitudes of strength.

For certain her parents never experienced such a feeling or such a being.

As the child grew, her intensity for life became more evident.

Sometimes in utter sweetness and affection and other times in the mischievous actions she took with relentless confidence.

As she grew older perhaps the parents forgot the beauty of this gift that the divine/the unknown had allowed to enter their lives.

She was a gift for herself and only herself to discover!

In time she would and she will time and time again.

Back to the story now, the parents consumed with their own life experiences and pain didn't pay attention to her needs, wants and the depth of longing for love that she needed, craved or wanted from her parents. She needed this from only her parents, her first humans no one else. If the parents were embracing this girl as their own then she was also viewing her parents as her own. She knew of no one else but them however they knew so many other humans. Perhaps never getting to actually know her. Going from a home to a house can be difficult; the journey from the womb to the world.

People are like this though and in this story it is no different. The parents overwhelmed by their own lives forgot how they nurtured the child when she was in the womb. Forgot how much raw affection they had previously shown. Forgot how much excitement they had at the idea of a baby girl! Does all the affection and care end when the child physically enters the world? Let us see. In many ways than one this girl grew up in her life time without unconditional support and unconditional love. She began to learn from herself and her experiences.

It seemed her parents didn't understand the power of emotions. Neglect is neglected in memory. Slowly she began loving herself in ways that she knew. Soon she met others outside of her first humans; outside of what she considered her world. How strange she thought these humans were, all of them! But no different than her first humans either I guess.
All with their purposes and ambitions. Some humans eternally

stuck in the mind,never living in the moments that were moving like the ground underneath their feet. Just like the ground that moves on this planet in this universe round and round rotating in the mystical circle unaware of this movement; so were other humans also unaware of the moments in their lives and that of others.

The girl noticed and observed all of this.

The girl continued to create her own world of exuberant unhindered joy in this paradox of a world. The girl became a woman. Becoming a woman can be traumatic. Becoming a woman she learned the rules of the world and realized the overarching influence that men had on every aspect of societal life. Men that should be labeled as boys because clearly there is widespread underdevelopment in the understanding of living an existence outside of control. She could not walk down the street without the unwanted gaze of a man; men of all ages. The inherent violence and disrespect present in each of these unwanted encounters. All of this was experienced at the tender age of sixteen; reminiscing adolescence before womanhood had fully come. How shameful she thought these men must be to not realize the abuse she and other women face just by existing!

The eyes which were given by the divine to see clarity of sight were in fact clouded and blinded in most of the men she encountered walking in this lifetime. Yet this did not stop her from

innocence

accessing the joy that she was gifted from the divine time and time again. She remained grateful for her existence and life regardless of how much space had passed between when she first came here.

She thought to herself, wouldn't it be beautiful if the humans in this world could just live freely? Where every human, including I of the woman's species was truly free?

So she harnessed the magic of being and let it explode into the world. As if the clouds above had burst with wild monsoon rain. Even the sky surrendered to the might of this woman. After all god isn't a man yet neither a woman. How could the sky not surrender? The rain that poured as a gift of surrender nurtured all of the life that would continue to enkindle the fire within all of creation. In spreading her warmth of compassion to herself naturally all those that resided on this planet began to heal.

Slowly surrendering.

Like this the norms of what was accepted as normal became disturbed yet peace roamed freely alongside.

It roamed freely until the men in the next generation stole the gift that this woman had given to the woman's race.

Even then another Supna came bringing with her the magic that brought her and every single one before her into this world.

Soo the dance continues for eternity.

innocence

**Fuck authority**

Never have I surrendered control to others just because of their titles or associations.

Where I come from you earn your respect

You don't just receive it

I will give you courtesy for the time being but respect is not granted to those that disrespect the sacred with their mere presence.

Look me in my eyes

You aren't taking anything

Even death won't give you that access.

Sever anything and anyone that demands otherwise.

Primal stringed kite

that I cling

Then release

Finally at peace

## Now & Here

Now it is time to rebuild our selves and later our communities.

This book is for everyone.

Everyone needs to touch and hug their innocence and never let go.

Traveling to a depth of vulnerability that brings the experience of being surrendered in profound joy and gratitude for the breath we breathe after drowning in expectation that the next breathe would never come.

Stop being a victim and culprit of your own misunderstandings of your emotions and thoughts. Tame your mind and heart with your will.

Recognize the power of your breathe and the innocence that resides in it.

I promise you it will change your life.

It definitely has changed my life.

As men, women and complex human beings we must transform the suffering that we have created into healing.

End the societal suffering.

We only have a limited amount of time and space in this one life that is guaranteed for the moment. Every other one is promised yet never guaranteed.

Do you really want to spend the only time and space that
you may ever have invested in survival, societal suffering and its byproducts? Or do you want intimacy with yourself and the life that you will leave one day forever?

Feel the innocence

Everywhere

Now go give this book to someone

In need

Go!

This page is for safe and open

expressions & communications

Write, draw or do whatever brings your heart joy!
Enjoy!